Mimi and Moto's Magical Meteors

First Gear

For Meah

Text Copyright © 2021 Nancy Gerloff and Mark Augustyn. Illustration Copyright © 2023 Nancy Gerloff and Mark Augustyn. All rights reserved. No part of this book may be reproduced in any manner whatsoever without written permission except in the case of brief quotations embodied in critical articles and reviews. Published in the United States by Little Rider Enterprises. Mimi and Moto is a registered trademark of Little Rider Enterprises.

www.mimiandmoto.com

ISBN 978-1-7379974-1-2 (hardcover)

Created, written, illustrated, and printed in the United States.
10 9 8 7 6 5 4 3 2 1

MIMI AND MOTO'S MAGICAL METEORS
FIRST GEAR

By Nancy Gerloff and Mark Augustyn

Illustrated and Designed by Esteban Alvarado

Little Rider Enterprises - Atlanta

CONTENTS

Chapter 1 7

Chapter 2 10

Chapter 3 14

Chapter 4 20

Chapter 5 28

Chapter 6 38

Chapter 7 45

Chapter 8 55

Chapter 9 63

Chapter 10 71

Chapter 11 82

Chapter 12 92

Chapter 13 100

Chapter 14 107

About the Authors 114

CHAPTER 1

The magical meteor made of motorcycles raced through space faster and faster and faster. As it zoomed past the planet Saturn, two monkeys were playing back on Mother Earth. They were swinging and jumping and running and giggling under the warm and cozy sunshine.

The monkeys had no idea that a magical meteor made of motorcycles was heading straight for Mother Earth. They also had no idea that it was about to turn their lives into an amazing two-wheel adventure.

After passing Saturn and its rings, only the ginormous planet Jupiter and the rusty red

planet Mars stood between it and Mother Earth. "Vroooom" was the sound it would make if there was sound in space. But as everyone knows, there is no sound in deep space, so the magical meteor made of motorcycles raced through space silently.

Where did the mysterious magical meteor made of motorcycles come from? Was it sent by motorcycle riding aliens from a nearby galaxy who ran out of storage space on their home planet? Or did it come from the far reaches of the universe, near a massive black hole, where time and space and motorcycles blended into one?

In the end, it did not matter who sent it or where it came from. What mattered was that a magical meteor made of motorcycles was speeding quickly through the solar system. Once it passed Jupiter and Mars, it slowly became visible from Mother Earth.

CHAPTER 2

The girl monkey was the first to notice something strange up in the great blue sky. It was nothing but a flicker in her eye, but her eyes were young and strong and focused. She knew that something was up there and it was moving fast, real fast. Whatever it was, it was not normal and she could not take her eyes off of it.

The boy monkey noticed her staring up at the sky so he looked up and saw it too. Something was definitely up there in the great blue sky, and it was moving fast, real fast.

The monkeys looked at each other. They were frozen in amazement because the object high up

in the great blue sky was also getting bigger. If it was getting bigger that meant it was getting closer. And if it was getting closer to Mother Earth, then it was getting closer to them!

The two monkeys were hypnotized by the mysterious object high up in the great blue sky. They had no idea that it was a magical meteor made of motorcycles. And they certainly had no idea that it would soon make them happier than they could have ever possibly imagined.

But before that happened, the magical meteor made of motorcycles started blocking out the sun. Slowly, daytime turned into nighttime. Thrown into a growing darkness, the two monkeys held their breath and held each other tightly. As the sun disappeared, all the animals, from the smallest to the tallest, huddled together and waited anxiously.

But a strange thing happened just before the meteor arrived. There was an amazing sound. It was heard all throughout the jungle. In fact, the sound was heard around the whole world.

It was a miraculous sound unlike any sound ever heard on Mother Earth before. It was not the sound of your average, every day, regular old meteor speeding towards Mother Earth.

Instead, the sound heard by all the animals that day on Mother Earth was the amazing roar of motorcycles.

CHAPTER 3

The two monkeys opened their eyes the next day at the exact same time. The bright yellow morning sun had just come up over the eastern horizon. It was shining on their cute little monkey faces through a window. They sat up in their beds and stared at each other.

They were not high up in their tree-top jungle home as they normally were when they woke up. Instead, they were in a bedroom in a small house. Sitting next to their beds, neatly arranged on the nightstand and floor next to them, were motorcycle helmets, gloves, and boots. On the wall above their beds hung a picture of the moon and the stars. "Moto, what happened?" blurted out the girl monkey.

She surprised herself. She had never spoken like this before now. She had never thought like this before now come to think of it. She had certainly never called the boy monkey by a name before but calling him 'Moto' felt right.

"Mimi, I have no clue what happened," the boy monkey replied while rubbing his eyes.

He surprised himself just like she did. He had never called her by a name before or even thought like this before. But just like Mimi, Moto could not ignore how good everything felt this morning. He liked speaking like this. He liked thinking like this. He liked the way 'Mimi' sounded so in his mind, Mimi she would be.

"The last thing I remember was holding you just before the meteor hit. I was trying to figure out where that roar was coming from and what it sounded like," Moto said.

"I heard the roar too! Did the meteor really

make that sound?" Mimi asked.

"It must have. I do not know how we fell asleep and ended up in this house, but I bet that meteor had something to do with it too. We should go outside, find out what happened and ride around," he added.

"Ride around?" Mimi asked.

They paused and stared at each other again. After a few seconds, Mimi started giggling.

"That sounds like a great idea. I would love to ride around. But what exactly are we going to ride around on?" she asked curiously.

Without saying another word, the monkeys got up out of bed. They grabbed the motorcycle gear near their beds and put it all on. Though this was their very first time, it felt as if they had put the gear on many times before.

When they opened the front door, the monkeys could not believe their eyes. It was simply amazing. Parked outside of their front door were motorcycles, lots and lots of motorcycles. The sun was reflecting off of them, sending rays of sunlight in every direction. It made the shiny motorcycles look like giant sparklers. The sight was so dazzling the monkeys had to squint their eyes just to see.

There was every kind of motorcycle you could imagine. There were dirtbikes, sportbikes, choppers, and cruisers. To the left were cafe-racers, adventure bikes, touring bikes, and some hill-climbers. To the right were sidecars, vintage motorcycles, and electric motorcycles. And behind all of these were pit bikes, trials bikes, and even a few ratty looking rat bikes.

Curiously, there were two of each kind of motorcycle, one slightly taller, one slightly shorter. Mimi and Moto looked at each other and giggled some more. While checking out all the motorcycles, Moto noticed something in the playground across the street. "Mimi, look, over there! It's a meteor and it's made of motorcycles!"

The monkeys ran as fast as they could across

the street to take a closer look. The magical meteor made of motorcycles was still smoking and shooting sparks high into the air. It had landed right next to the monkey bars which made both Mimi and Moto laugh. Packed so tightly with motorcycles, it was impossible to see any light coming through the meteor. There were motorcycle parts laying all over the ground.

"Well, now we know for sure what the sound was yesterday. It was definitely the roar of motorcycles," said a smiling Moto.

Things did not make complete sense, but at least they made a little more sense now. The meteor was magical and it was made of motorcycles. After crashing into Mother Earth yesterday, it changed everything overnight. The monkeys had been magically transformed. They were now Mimi and Moto, the monkeys who love motorcycles.

CHAPTER 4

Mimi and Moto looked at each other. Without saying a word, they knew what needed to happen next. It was time to go on their first ever motorcycle ride.

The monkeys walked back across the street to look at all the motorcycles more closely. They crossed their little monkey arms, stood back, and marveled at all the beautiful machines standing in front of them.

"I don't know why, but I love all of these motorcycles. I want to ride each one of them," proclaimed Mimi confidently.

"Me too!" added Moto excitedly.

There was just one tiny problem. Neither Mimi nor Moto actually knew how to ride a motorcycle. Or at least they thought they did not know how to ride.

"How do you think we should get started?" Mimi asked.

"I think we need to trust the power of the magical meteor made of motorcycles. Do you remember learning how to swing from a tree with your tail?" asked Moto.

"No, of course not," replied Mimi. "We're monkeys and swinging from trees with our tails comes to us naturally. It's called 'instinct'." She always enjoyed using smart words.

"Ok, well, since the magical meteor made of motorcycles crashed so close to us, and since we woke up in this new motorcycle world, I think we need to just trust our instincts," replied Moto. The two monkeys looked at all the motorcycles. They were trying to decide which ones to ride first. Suddenly, two motorcycles parked in front of the playground started up on their own. The monkeys looked at each other and started laughing. The magical meteor made of motorcycles was trying to give them a hint.

"Mimi look, the green color of the taller motorcycle matches my helmet," said Moto excitedly.

"I love it! And look, the shorter blue one matches the racing stripe on my helmet," noted Mimi.

When they walked up to the motorcycles, the engines were purring like happy cats. They put on their helmets which felt warm and safe. They put on their gloves which fit their little monkey hands perfectly. Their boots, already on, felt solid and secure on their feet. They swung their legs over the seats, grabbed the handlebars, adjusted their tails, and sat down.

"Moto, I don't know how this is supposed to feel, but I think this motorcycle fits me perfectly. What about you?"

"Mine feels great too," replied Moto. He paused for a few seconds and then added, "I think I was born to ride motorcycles."

"What did you just say?" Mimi asked.

Moto repeated slowly, "I said it feels like I was born to ride motorcycles."

"I was just thinking the exact same thing," said Mimi grinning.

The monkeys smiled at each other and twisted the throttles. The engines roared. The sound was incredible. It reminded them of the roar they heard yesterday just before the magical meteor made of motorcycles crashed into the playground.

With each twist of the throttle, Mimi and Moto felt the engines vibrate underneath them. It felt like they were sitting on small, rumbling volcanoes getting ready to explode.

"I think it's time Mimi. Let's ride!" shouted Moto over the sound of the motorcycles.

Side by side, Mimi and Moto cautiously

made their way down the street heading away from the playground. Behind them, the magical meteor made of motorcycles started shooting off more sparks as if it was excited for the monkeys too.

Before they got to the end of the street, any doubts they had about riding quickly faded away. The magical meteor made of motorcycles had completely transformed them. They were not just monkeys who magically woke up loving motorcycles. They were now monkeys who could actually ride motorcycles.

Turning right at the end of the street, Mimi and Moto saw the road heading off into the distance. It was wide open so they twisted the throttles and sped up.

They instantly felt the warm breeze against their furry little bodies. Their little monkey noses could smell everything they passed, including the trees, the flowers, the rivers, even the grass. Their eyes were seeing the world for the first time

as motorcycle riders and they loved what they saw. Adventure and excitement seemed to be everywhere. Who knew that being a motorcycle rider was so cool and so awesome!

Mimi and Moto were smiling like they had never smiled before. Mimi thought her smile might be stuck on her face permanently. Moto thought he might actually break his face from smiling so hard.

The two of them were having so much fun on their first ride that they completely lost track of time. The sun, which was high up in the great blue sky when they started, was now sinking quickly towards the western horizon.

Then something unexpected happened. The motorcycles, which had been running perfectly all day, started to burp and chirp and cough as if they were suddenly sick. Unsure of what was going on, Mimi and Moto carefully pulled over to the side of the road. When they did, both motorcycles sputtered and shut off. Everything became quiet suddenly.

Mimi shook her head while taking off her helmet. "I know this sounds crazy, but I think I know what the problem is."

"Let me guess, you don't know how you know, but you think we ran out of gas, right?" asked Moto.

"Exactly!" Mimi shot back as they both checked their gas tanks. "Yep. My tank is empty."

"Mine too," confirmed Moto. He paused then asked, "So what are we going to do now? We have no gas. We have not seen a gas station. We are here out in the middle of nowhere. And it's getting dark quickly."

Mimi did not know what to say, which was weird. She always seemed to have an answer for him, but this time she did not. Moto did not know what to say either and he continued looking worried. The monkeys sat silently on the side of the road wondering what to do next.

CHAPTER 5

After a few minutes by the side of the road, Mimi and Moto heard an engine off in the distance. They looked up and saw two lights coming down the road towards them.

"I think it is a car," said Moto.

However, once the lights came closer, they realized it was not a car. It was two motorcycles. The two riders pulled up and turned off their engines. There were tails behind each rider and whiskers poking out of their helmets. One tail was narrow and neat. The other animal's tail was fluffy and puffy.

When the two motorcycle riders pulled off

their helmets, Mimi and Moto could not believe their eyes. Smiling back at them was a cat and a dog. As the pair walked up to the monkeys, they noticed that the dog was carrying a gas can.

"Well, hello there fellow motorcycle riders," said the cat while straightening out her whiskers. "Looks like we got here just in time. Got yourselves in a bit of trouble, yes-meow?"

Mimi and Moto were astonished at what they were seeing and hearing. Up until today, the only cats they knew of were ferocious lions and fierce tigers who usually just wanted to eat monkeys. They stood in place watching the cat. She walked up to their motorcycles, rubbed her fur on them, and purred softly.

"What's the matter? Cat got your tongue-woof?" asked the dog. He laughed so hard his long ears flipped and flopped back and forth. They looked like giant bed sheets blowing and dancing in the wind.

"There is no reason to be afraid. My best

friend forever does not want to eat you. She is the sweetest motorcycle riding cat you will ever meet. A little too smarty pants sometimes but I'm used to it-ruff," said the dog with a smile.

Still speechless, Mimi and Moto watched the dog carefully fill up both of their tanks. He did not spill a single drop of gas. Once finished, the dog proudly stepped back from the motorcycles. He pulled a large bone from his jacket, laid down, and started to chew on it.

The cat gracefully jumped up and stood on the monkeys' motorcycles. She placed a paw on each gas tank. With eyes and jaws wide open, Mimi and Moto gazed up at her.

"I am so, so sorry. We did not properly introduce ourselves. My name is Bella K. Kat but you can just call me Bella. The K stands for Kitty of course. This is my best friend forever and partner in riding, Bailey F. Fido. If you are curious, the F stands for Frank-meow." She licked her paws, stroked her whiskers again, and kept talking as cats often do. "We are from a small village, just over the mountain that sits at the far northern edge of what used to be your jungle. You did come from the jungle, yes-meow?"

Mimi and Moto nodded their heads silently. Bailey looked up, nodded his head, and happily went back to chewing on his bone.

"Can you talk too-meow?" Bella asked.

"Yes, we can t-t-talk," Moto said nervously.

"Excellent, because Bailey and I do not speak a lick of your monkey language," Bella said with a laugh. "And until waking up this morning, we've only meowed and barked at each other. This talking thing sure is helpful-meow."

Mimi and Moto smiled at each other. The initial shock of seeing Bella and Bailey was fading away fast.

"My name is Mimi and this is Moto." She went on and explained what had happened to them since the magical meteor made of motorcycles appeared yesterday. Bella listened while still balanced on the motorcycles like a gymnast.

Mimi immediately liked Bella. She liked her style. She sounded smart with a healthy dash of sassy. Mimi had heard that cats are survivors and have nine lives. She suspected Bella had already lived quite a few of her cat lives. Maybe that is why she sounded so wise. Mimi had a feeling that they could become best friends forever too.

Bella jumped off their motorcycles skillfully and landed right next to Bailey. She snatched the bone from his snout and tossed it as far as she could. Bailey shot off like a rocket and retrieved the bone. He growled at Bella playfully and then returned to his place near the motorcycles. Bella sat down next to him and started licking her paws.

"Do you two want to actually see the magical meteor made of motorcycles?" Moto asked.

Bella stopped her licking to look up at him. Bailey dropped the bone, shook his floppy ears, and looked right at Moto too.

"You know where it is-woof?" the dog asked.

"We sure do. The meteor landed in a playground across the street from our new house. It's made up of thousands, maybe millions of motorcycles packed together tightly," Moto told the pair.

"Can we see it-woof?! Do you know how to get to it-ruff?!" barked Bailey while jumping up and down excitedly.

"Of course. It's back down the road that way," answered Moto. He pointed in the direction of where they had come from. Bailey looked back down the road and sniffed the air.

"Hmm, I think I can smell it. Let's go-ruff-ruff-ruff!" barked Bailey at the top of his lungs.

They needed to ride back to the magical meteor made of motorcycles before it got completely dark. Carefully, they put their helmets and gloves back on. Inside their helmets, each animal was smiling from ear to ear. They knew it was going to be a great ride and they were excited.

Without any warning, Bella stopped and quickly looked up. She arched her back. Her cat fur stood up. She was trying hard to listen to something. Bella always heard things before Bailey. She looked up the road. The rest of the animals looked at her.

Whispering, Bailey asked, "Bella, what do you hear-woof?"

"An engine-meow," she replied suspiciously.

"Yay, we get to meet more motorcycle riding animals!" Moto shouted. Mimi got excited too.

They saw two lights come over the hill and down the road in their direction. It reminded the monkeys of when they first saw Bella and Bailey's headlights.

Mimi and Moto and Bailey were sure it was two more motorcycles. But Bella was not so sure. Her cat ears were extremely good and she could hear better than the others. She kept trying to hear two engines but could only hear one.

"Something is definitely not right-meow,"

Bella announced with a serious tone in her voice.

As the lights got closer, the animals realized they were not two motorcycles. The lights were just one car. It was swerving wildly back and forth across the road like a snake.

As quickly as they could, the animals jumped on their motorcycles. They had only a few seconds left and wanted to keep themselves and their motorcycles safe. They had to act fast, real fast.

They moved quickly and hid behind some huge trees growing on both sides of the road. For the moment, they would be safe.

The car flew by them as they watched from behind the trees. It was an ugly looking little car. It was covered with rusty spots that made it look like it was old and sick. Thick black smoke poured out of the exhaust pipe like a chimney.

Two large heads with hats on them were poking out of the sunroof of the car. The arms connected to the heads were huge and hairy. The bodies connected to the arms were enormous and oozed out the windows of the car. The driver and passenger were packed in like sardines in a can. They were far too large for the ugly little car.

After it passed, the monkeys sniffed the air. There was an animal scent they both recognized immediately. Mimi looked at Moto. Moto looked at Mimi. Bella and Bailey looked at Mimi and Moto.

The two monkeys screamed, "Oh no! Gorillas!"

CHAPTER 6

"Hurry up! Come on!" shouted Mimi. "They are heading towards the magical meteor made of motorcycles!" Mimi knew something was wrong the moment she saw the gorillas driving the car.

Mimi and Moto and Bella and Bailey pulled their motorcycles from behind the trees and back onto the road. They started chasing the car. Despite the thick black smoke, they were able to read the license plate on the back of the ugly little car. It said: THE CAGES.

The four animals needed to come up with a plan. But doing so while chasing the Cages would be impossible. If they stopped, the gorillas would get away. And if they got away, they might get to the magical meteor made of motorcycles first.

Not sure what to do, Moto started talking to himself inside his helmet, "I can't believe this is happening. Why are two gorillas driving a car?!"

With nothing to lose and everything to gain, he decided to try asking the magical meteor made of motorcycles for help.

"Hey meteor, if you can hear me, we need your help fast, real fast! We need to stop two gorillas in a car before they get to you. We think they may try to harm you. If you are as magical as I think you are, please send me a sign in three, two, one..."

The words floated into his head instantly. Moto could not tell if he was hearing them, thinking them, or imagining them.

"Moto, I can hear you, I can hear you! Can you hear me? It's Mimi. Look over here! Look, look, look!"

When Moto turned to look, Mimi's helmet

was glowing. She gave him a thumbs up. The magical meteor made of motorcycles had heard him.

"Mimi, your helmet is glowing blue! I can hear you perfectly inside my helmet. The meteor is helping us. We can talk to each other!"

"I know Moto, I know! Your helmet is glowing green! It's amazing! Bella? Bailey? This is Mimi. Can you hear us?"

The monkeys instantly heard meowing and barking inside their helmets. They peeked over their shoulders. Bella and Bailey's helmets were glowing too. Bella's glow was pink, Bailey's was golden.

"We hear you loud and clear monkeys-meow!"

"Now let's go and protect the magical meteor made of motorcycles from the Cages-ruff!"

It was incredible. Mimi and Moto and Bella and Bailey could magically talk to each other inside their helmets while riding. But they had no time to waste marveling at their new magical power.

With great care and skill, they moved to the left and quickly passed the Cage's ugly little car. They were glad to be out of the thick black smoke. When they looked back in their mirrors, they could see that the gorilla driving was angry and beating on his hairy chest.

Now in front of the Cage's car, they sped up even more. The gorillas tried staying close behind but could not quite catch up to the motorcycles. The exhaust pipe was spitting out even more thick black smoke.

"Moto, we're about to come up to that big intersection we passed earlier. Remember? We should split up there and see if the Cages will follow one of us away from the playground."

"Great idea Mimi. Bella and Bailey, did you hear that? Are you ready?"

"Copy that, yes-meow!"

"Yessiree-woof!"

As they came around a curve, they could see the intersection Mimi was talking about. Moto and Bailey leaned and turned left at the intersection. Mimi and Bella leaned and turned right. But the Cages did not turn at all. They continued driving their ugly little car straight forward.

Mimi yelled inside her helmet, *"Everyone, turn around! Turn around now! Our plan didn't work. Get back to the main road. We have to catch back up to the gorillas!"*

The four of them turned around. It did not take long to catch back up to the Cage's car. The trail of thick black smoke was easy to see with their headlights. Up ahead, there were sparks shooting high into the air over the trees.

Mimi and Moto immediately knew why the Cages had not turned to follow them. They were heading for the sparks. This meant they were heading towards the playground. This was not good at all.

"Can you hear me magical meteor made of motorcycles? This is Mimi. You need to stop shooting sparks into the air right now! The gorillas are heading towards you. We don't know what they're going to do but we're worried. Please stop sparking!"

As soon as Mimi stopped talking, the meteor stopped sparking. The Cage's car slowed down. The gorillas were not sure where to go. Mimi and Moto and Bella and Bailey slowed their motorcycles down too.

"Thanks magical meteor made of motor cycles. Ok everyone, we don't have much time," yelled Mimi. *"The gorillas are confused so let them go. Follow me to the playground now!"*

CHAPTER 7

Leading the way and trusting her instincts, Mimi leaned her motorcycle and took a hard left turn. The others followed her. The four animals in their glowing helmets raced from one street to the next. After two more quick right turns and one left turn, she had it figured out. The four furry friends pulled right up to the playground.

Mimi and Moto and Bella and Bailey got off their motorcycles and took off their gear. They quickly hid everything behind the magical meteor made of motorcycles where it would not be seen.

They gathered up sticks, branches, leaves, and

anything else they could find. Their plan was to camouflage it. After a few minutes, the magical meteor made of motorcycles was completely covered. The monkeys were glad it was now dark. The playground lights would cast lots of shadows. This would help to confuse the Cages even more.

As they finished, they could hear the gorillas' car coming. Bailey could already smell its thick black smoke. The ugly little car turned the corner and slowly made its way down the street towards the playground.

Mimi whispered, "Everyone, act natural."

The monkeys hopped up on the monkey bars. They used their tails and started swinging back and forth. Then they jumped onto the magical meteor made of motorcycles. Careful not to uncover it, they then jumped onto a nearby tree. Without their motorcycle gear on, they looked like normal monkeys just playing and having fun high above the ground.

The cat and dog were doing their part too. Bella swiped her paw at Bailey's nose and took off running. Bailey chased after her. Round and round they went circling the covered up magical meteor made of motorcycles.

From the corners of their eyes, the four of them watched for the Cage's car. It slowly came up to the playground. They were hoping that their little show would fool the gorillas.

When the car stopped, Moto almost screamed. Mimi's tail almost slipped off the monkey bars. Bella and Bailey opened their eyes wider than wide and stared at the ugly little car. Had the Cages seen through their charade? Did the gorillas see a piece of the magical meteor made of motorcycles?

From the ugly little car Mr. Cage looked at the playground and grunted, "I can't stand happy, little, pesky monkeys jumping around." He looked annoyed because he was annoyed. He scrunched his nose as if he smelled something awful. This made his face look like a fist. Slowly, he started driving the ugly little car away.

From the passenger seat Mrs. Cage timidly asked, "Uh, why do we not like, um, um, pesky monkeys again?"

"I don't know! We just don't. Now be quiet and let me drive. Just keep looking for the sparks and those four motorcycles," Mr. Cage shouted back.

Mrs. Cage stayed quiet and laughed to herself. She dared not say that she thought the monkeys looked cute and adorable.

When the Cages drove away, Mimi and Moto and Bella and Bailey each let out a sigh of relief. They kept their show going on for just a little longer. They watched until the ugly little car drove out of sight. When they could no longer hear it, they ended their little playground performance.

"Wow, that was close," said Moto. "I was sure they had figured out that we were just pretending

and trying to trick them."

"Great job everyone," replied Mimi.

"Thanks, but where is Bailey-meow?" asked Bella.

In their excitement, no one had noticed that the dog had disappeared.

"Bailey? Bailey, where are you-meow?" called Bella.

"Back here-ruff," said Bailey from the other side of the magical meteor made of motorcycles. "Everyone, come here! You have got to see this-woof."

When they went around, they found Bailey staring at a spot on the magical meteor made of motorcycles.

"While I was chasing Bella, I kept seeing this shiny spot right here-woof," he said pointing his paw at it.

There was something bolted to the side of the magical meteor made of motorcycles. It was a large, shiny, flat metal plate. Bailey had already removed the leaves, sticks, and branches covering it. The shiny metal plate had scratch marks on it left there from its long journey through space. It had words engraved into it that were clear and readable:

**OUR MAGICAL METEORS
MADE OF MOTORCYCLES
ARE YOURS TO GUARD AND PROTECT.
UNTIL THE DAY WE MEET,
WE OWE YOU MUCH RESPECT.**

The animals stood there studying the words. Each looked up at the sky and thought about who or what had written the message. Even though it was another mystery to add to their growing list of mysteries, the words made them feel good.

Mimi and Moto and Bella and Bailey looked at each other and smiled. Their first day as motorcycle riders had been amazing. Using the sticks, branches, and leaves he had removed,

Bailey again covered the shiny metal plate.

"Ok everyone, let's get some rest. Bella and Bailey, you can sleep on our floor. I think the magical meteor made of motorcycles will be safe for the night. And since the Cages are still looking for us, Mimi and I are going to set up a little meteor magic trick to scare them away," said Moto.

***

After leaving the playground, the Cages kept looking for sparks and the motorcycle riders. It was getting later and later. Mrs. Cage started to worry while Mr. Cage turned down another street.

When he did, they both looked up to see a huge, illuminated billboard sign. It was staring down at them with huge neon letters on it. The gorillas came to a sudden stop in the middle of the street. They read the sign together which said:

WELCOME TO THE ZOO

Mr. Cage slammed his foot on the gas as hard as he could. Mrs. Cage's head bounced against her seat. The car's tires squealed and left thick black marks on the road.

They did not know where they were going. Nor did they care where they were going. The gorillas just wanted to get away as fast as their ugly little car could take them. Zoos made gorillas very, very nervous. Searching for the source of the sparks and the four motorcycle riders would have to wait until tomorrow.

If the Cages had turned around, they would have seen how the zoo sign faded away and magically disappeared.

***

Back at the house across the street from the playground, all was quiet. The four furry friends were now sound asleep. They were dreaming about motorcycle adventures.

Mimi and Moto were in their comfortable beds. Bailey was laying on his back with all four legs sticking straight up in the air. His tongue was hanging out. He was snoring loudly. Bella was curled up in a ball and sleeping soundly on his stomach. She was used to Bailey's loud snoring and liked his soft belly.

When the Cage's car sped away from the magical disappearing zoo sign, Mimi and Moto rolled over in their beds and stretched. Small, sleepy smiles broke out on each monkey's face. Before falling asleep, they had magically placed the floating zoo sign on the side of the road. Their little magic trick had worked just as they had planned. The magical meteor made of motorcycles would be safe for tonight. But tomorrow would be a completely different story.

CHAPTER 8

Mimi and Moto slowly opened their eyes the next day. The bright yellow morning sun was shining through their window again. As the monkeys rubbed the sleepiness from their eyes, they heard a buzzing sound outside. It sounded like a swarm of bees going back and forth.

When they sat up to look, they saw a large dark creature standing inside their room. It was looking out their window. The creature was casting a long and dark shadow across their beds. The monkeys did not move a muscle.

They could not tell what it was. It looked like an alien from outer space that was large and furry. It had two tails. The tail at the bottom of its body was fluffy and puffy. The second tail was narrow and neat and attached to the creature's neck. Both tails were swaying together from side to side. It slowly started to turn its head. Mimi and Moto pulled their bed sheets up so only their eyes were visible. Then the creature started to speak.

"Oh, the sweepy wittle monkeys are finawy awake?" said Bella jokingly. "We thought you would never wake up. Come over here and look at this now-meow!"

Mimi and Moto relaxed and giggled. The dark creature standing at their window was not an alien from outer space after all. It was Bella sitting on top of Bailey's head. They pulled their bed sheets back and got up to look out the window.

Outside their front door, they saw small motorcycles zipping back and forth. This explained the buzzing sound they had heard.

Sitting atop each little motorcycle was a raccoon wearing goggles, a helmet, gloves, boots, and a cute, little leather vest.

"One, two, three, four," said Mimi as she counted the riding raccoons. "Twelve, thirteen, fourteen. Yep, there are fourteen raccoons out there."

"What does it say on the back of their leather vests-woof?" asked Bailey.

Trying to get a better look, Bella replied, "I think it says Bandits and Gazers-meow."

"What does that mean? Is it some kind of riddle-ruff?" asked Bailey.

"Wait a minute," chimed in Moto, "I think I know. Raccoons look like bandits because of the black fur around their eyes. And a large group of raccoons is known as a 'gaze'."

The four furry friends opened the front door and stepped outside. The raccoons came to a stop. They turned off their motorcycles and lifted up their goggles.

It was a magical site to see. Two monkeys, a cat, and a dog standing face to face with fourteen motorcycle riding raccoons. In the blink of an eye, the raccoons jumped up and stood on their motorcycles. Together, they recited a poem:

We love to ride motorcycles, especially at night.
For our eyes work better when there is no light.
Our job is to help, assist and warn
Our motorcycle riding animal friends
Of danger and scorn.
For there are two gorillas who now drive a car.
And we are here to tell you that they are not far.
They are coming back to find and steal
The magical meteor made of two-wheels.
Our warning is real, so we ask you to heed,
Every word we utter before we must leave.
Prepare and be ready for time is short,
The gorillas are coming back again.
You have been warned.
Vroom, vroom!

The Bandits and Gazers put their goggles back on and sat on their little motorcycles. The buzzing of the engines starting up sounded like a beehive again. One by one, the raccoons turned around and headed straight for the playground across the street.

"What are they doing?" asked a concerned and worried looking Mimi.

The first raccoon pulled a wheelie and rode straight up the slide using it like a ramp. It looked like it was going to jump off of it. But instead, the raccoon did a back-flip, floated in the air for a second, and then magically shot off towards the clouds. The remaining thirteen raccoons followed and did the same exact thing.

The raccoons looked like fireworks shooting off into the sky. Each one left a brightly colored trail of smoke floating in the air. The colors were the same as each raccoon's motorcycle. By the time the last raccoon jumped off, there were fourteen trails of colored smoke heading off in different directions across the great blue sky.

"Now that was cool-woof!" barked Bailey.

"Do you think we will see them again-meow?" asked Bella.

Mimi and Moto looked at each other and smiled.

"We think so," said Moto. "Remember their poem? They said their job was to help other motorcycle riding animal friends. I'm sure they will be back."

This made Bella even more curious. "Do you think we are the raccoon's only motorcycle riding animal friends? Or are there more animals like us now riding motorcycles-meow?"

"We're not sure. Maybe. Maybe not. It's another mystery we'll have to figure out. But now is not the time," added Mimi. "They warned us that the gorillas were close by. We need to think fast and get ready."

As soon as the words left her mouth, Bailey ran to the edge of the street. He started barking.

He was looking at something. The other three ran over to get a better look themselves.

Off in the distance, over the mountain, and above the trees, they could see a plume of smoke rising into the air. It was thick and black. As they watched, the smoke appeared to be moving slowly from right to left. Each of the animals stared at it and each knew exactly what it was. Only Bailey with his strong nose could actually smell it.

"It's the gorillas and they are on the move again-r-r-r-r-ruff," growled Bailey.

"Uh oh," muttered Mimi.

"Uh oh is right," replied Moto.

The last thing Mimi and Moto wanted to do was to wait around for the gorillas to come back. They could not keep the magical meteor made of motorcycles covered up forever. If it started sparking again for any reason, the gorillas would find out where it was. They needed to come up with a plan to stop the Cages.

CHAPTER 9

On the other side of the mountain, Mr. and Mrs. Cage were driving along a bumpy dirt road. Their ugly little car was bouncing all over the place and making terrible noises. It sounded like it was about to fall apart. With each bump, the gorillas' heads went up and down as if they were on a carnival ride.

"I told you not to take this dirt road," shouted Mrs. Cage. "Watch out for that branch! You are going too fast. Slow down. Ouch, my knees! Do you know where you are going? I told you to slow down! Why don't you ever listen to me? I told you the sparks we saw came from the other side of the mountain. Ouch, ouch! Slow down!"

With each comment, Mr. Cage grew angrier and angrier and angrier. He remembered getting upset when he was still in the jungle, but not like this. Never in his life was he as angry as he was right now sitting behind the wheel of their ugly little car.

He gripped the steering wheel even tighter. His brown knuckles started to turn white. He knew he had made a mistake but did not want to admit it. As Mrs. Cage continued shouting in his ear, Mr. Cage's rage grew and grew and grew until he could not take it any longer.

The ugly little car came to a sudden stop. Mr. Cage jumped out of the car and started beating his chest with both fists. He roared and grunted so loud that the nearby trees shook.

Mr. Cage then ripped off his clothes and threw down his hat. He started running around the car on all fours. As he ran, he roared and grunted even more. He ripped branches off the trees.

Leaves were flying in every direction. He looked like a small tornado tearing up everything in its path.

Inside the ugly little car, Mrs. Cage was trying hard not to laugh out loud. She thought he looked like a horse galloping. She bit her lip. She pinched her arm. She looked down. She looked away as her beloved 'gorilla-nado' outside went round and round and round. She knew that if she laughed it would only make him angrier.

Eventually, Mr. Cage's temper tantrum ended and he calmed down. He wiped off the leaves and dust that had stuck to his fur. He found his clothes and put them back on. He dusted off his hat and put that back on too. He was back to his normal, dorky-looking gorilla self. He got back in the car and slammed the door.

"Well, I hope you feel better now," Mrs. Cage said calmly, still trying hard not to laugh at him.

Mr. Cage mumbled something under his breath. Mrs. Cage wisely decided not to ask him what he had said. The ugly little car turned around.

***

Back on the other side of the mountain, Mimi and Moto and Bella and Bailey had a new strategy. Instead of waiting for the Cages to come back in their direction, they would head towards the gorillas. It was a risky plan, but they had to try something.

To reach the gorillas, they would need to ride over the mountain on trails and dirt roads. The four furry friends ran back inside to get their motorcycle gear on.

"Hurry up everyone. We don't have much time. We need to get to the gorillas while they are still on the other side of the mountain," Moto said urgently.

"Why does all of our gear look different-woof?" asked Bailey.

"Yeah, look at my helmet. It's different too," added Bella. "It has this thing sticking out of it that looks like a bird's beak. My pants have different pads in them. These boots have a lot of buckles. My gloves are different too-meow."

"Looks like the magical meteor made of motorcycles heard our plan and is helping us with the right gear," replied Mimi.

The four furry friends finished gearing up and ran back out the front door. There they found four new motorcycles magically waiting for them. One was blue, one was green, one was pink, and one was gold. They were not the same motorcycles they had ridden yesterday.

"Wow, cool," exclaimed Mimi.

"Cool is right," added Moto.

"The tires look like they have teeth on them, and the fenders are bigger too-meow," observed Bella.

In the blink of an eye, they jumped on the motorcycles and started them. All of their helmets started glowing again. Led by Moto they took off, crossed the street, and zipped through the playground. The magical meteor made of motorcycles started shooting sparks high into the air.

In her glowing helmet, Mimi shouted, "No, no, no! Not now. No sparks. P-l-e-e-e-ease. The gorillas might see." The sparking stopped instantly.

Behind the playground, Moto saw a dirt trail heading up the mountain. He pointed his motorcycle at it, twisted the throttle, and pulled a small wheelie. The others followed him.

At the beginning of the trail was a small mound of dirt shaped like a ramp. Moto hit it, launching himself and his motorcycle into the air. He felt like a bird flying. "Weeeeeeee!" he shouted to himself.

One by one, the others also hit the small dirt ramp launching themselves into the air. And just like that, all four motorcycles disappeared and headed up the trail.

Their mission was simple. Find the gorillas

on the other side of the mountain and make sure they would not come back to the playground. The magical meteor made of motorcycles was depending on them.

CHAPTER 10

The trail going over the mountain zigged and zagged, back and forth, left and right. The sunlight was shining through the trees. This made some parts of the trail brighter and some parts darker. Scattered everywhere were branches, sticks, leaves, and rocks.

Moto, followed by Mimi and Bella and Bailey, formed a single file line. There was not enough room on the trail to ride side by side. The motorcycles bounced back and forth gracefully. Even though they were on a super-serious mission to find the gorillas, the four furry friends were having a blast riding up the trail.

Out front, Moto wanted to double check that they could still magically speak to each other inside their helmets.

"Mimi, Bella, Bailey. Can you hear me ok?"

"Yes Moto, I'm right behind you."

"Yep. I'm right here behind Mimi. Weeeeeee-meow.'

"Loud and clear from the rear-woof-woof-woof!"

"Excellent. Now just stay close. Once we get to the top of the mountain, we'll stop and look for the Cage's car."

They continued their two-wheel dance up the mountain. Their glowing helmets looked like bouncy balls bouncing up the trail. Kicked up by their tires, little bits of dirt and rock were flying behind them. When it became steeper, they slowed down and rode more carefully. Where the trail flattened out, they sped up. Who knew that protecting the magical meteor made of motorcycles could be so much fun!

Nearing the top, Moto slowed down as did the others. They knew the gorillas were on the other side of the mountain so they needed to be extra careful.

Moto quickly found a small clearing where they parked their motorcycles. They had a perfect view of the green valley below. They also had a perfect view of the gorilla's ugly little car. It was moving away from them down a dirt road. As usual, thick black smoke filled the air behind it.

"There they are. Look-look-ruff-ruff!" barked Bailey excitedly.

"What are we going to do now-meow?" added Bella.

"We have no time to waste. We can't lose them," shouted Moto.

"I agree, let's go. We can figure out our next move later," added Mimi.

In an instant, the four furry friends started riding down the other side of the mountain. The trail ended at the dirt road down below.

What they did not know was that the dirt road below led to a paved road. The paved road went back around the mountain and straight back to the playground. If the gorillas took a right onto the paved road, they would be heading back towards the magical meteor made of motorcycles. This would not be good at all.

At the bottom of the trail, Mimi and Moto and Bella and Bailey quickly turned right. They were now on the same dirt road they saw the gorillas driving on earlier.

All four animals were glad to be off the trail for the moment. Even though it was tons of fun, riding the trail over the mountain was hard work. The dirt road would be a nice break.

The Cage's ugly little car could not be too far ahead. They slowed down and stayed back to make sure the gorillas would not see or hear them. Like the trail over the mountain, rays of sunlight streamed down through the trees and shined on the dirt road. But as they continued, they noticed less thick black smoke. And around the next curve, they saw no smoke at all.

"Let's stop for a second. I can't see any more smoke. Can you make out anything Mimi?"

"No Moto, I can't. We have to watch out and not let the gorillas know we are following them."

They stopped their motorcycles in the middle of the dirt road. After taking their helmets off, they listened. Except for some birds chirping, they heard nothing.

"This is not good," said Moto. "We can't lose the gorillas now. If we do, the magical meteor made of motorcycles might be in trouble."

"But these motorcycles are a lot louder," added Mimi. "What if we get back on them and the Cages hear us?"

Bailey thought for a moment, scratched himself and then barked out, "I've got an idea! Listen up-woof-woof."

Bailey was the oldest of the four animals. He came from a champion bloodline of dogs. The other animals turned and listened to the wise old hound.

"If we can't see or smell their smoke, the Cages can't be far. Bella and I will go on a scouting mission-ruff."

"Go on, go on, tell us more," Moto added impatiently.

Bailey continued, "Bella and I will take off our motorcycle gear. We will look like a regular cat and dog just like yesterday at the playground. We'll run down the dirt road and I will pretend to be chasing Bella. Once we catch up to the Cages, we can see what is going on and then we'll come back. We fooled them last night so I'm sure we can fool them again-bow-wow."

"Brilliant idea." Mimi proclaimed. "Just remember, be quick and be careful," she added.

Bella and Bailey took off running. Bella took the lead while Bailey pretended to be chasing her. Before Mimi and Moto realized it, the cat and dog had disappeared down the dirt road.

They ran as fast as their cat and dog legs could take them. Bella and Bailey knew they had an important job to do. Each kept looking for any sign of the Cages.

Off in the distance, they could see where the dirt road ended. Once closer, they could see the gorilla's ugly little car parked on the side of the paved road.

Bella and Bailey headed straight for the gorillas' car. The Cages were standing on the other side of it. They were looking back at something behind the ugly little car. The cat and dog were so focused on playing their parts that they did not notice what the gorillas were looking at.

"Look, it's the cat and dog from the playground. How did they get here?" shouted Mr. Cage.

"Oh, how cute," replied Mrs. Cage.

"Cute?! Get a hold of yourself. If they come any closer, I will have to go and…"

"You will not do anything," Mrs. Cage snapped back, glaring at Mr. Cage. "I just love watching dogs chase cats. They are so adorable."

Bella and Bailey heard and understood every word the Cages were saying. Though Bella was tempted to say something smart-alecky, she knew better and kept running. The gorillas could not find out that they understood every word.

When Bella led Bailey around the front of the gorillas' ugly little car, she saw what the Cages had been looking at. She had to stop herself from screaming. When Bailey got around the front of the car and looked, he had to stop himself from screaming too. Doing so would have given them away so they kept running around the car.

To be extra convincing, Bella screeched wildly. Bailey barked as loud as he could. The Cages backed up. Mr. Cage looked as annoyed as ever. Mrs. Cage was trying to look annoyed, but actually had a little smile on her face. Both watched as the dog kept chasing the cat around their ugly little rusted car.

Bella and Bailey had seen everything they needed to see. Their mission was complete. They had to end their little show and get back to warn Mimi and Moto as soon as possible.

They stopped in front of the Cages one last time. Bella tried to scratch Bailey's nose. Bailey snarled back at Bella. And just as fast as they had appeared, they ran back down the dirt road and disappeared.

Back at the motorcycles, Mimi and Moto anxiously waited for the cat and dog to return.

"I can hear something," said Mimi.

"Me too. Look, here they come," Moto replied as Bella and Bailey came running down the dirt road.

The cat and dog ran up to Mimi and Moto. They were both breathing heavily and could barely speak.

"Well, what's going on? Did you find the gorillas?" Mimi asked impatiently.

Bella and Bailey explained that they found the Cages and had seen two trailers parked on both sides of the road. One trailer was carrying a huge crane. The other trailer was carrying a large bulldozer.

"Oh no," replied Moto.

CHAPTER II

In the middle of the dirt road, Bella and Bailey began to put their motorcycle gear back on. Mimi and Moto started talking about what they should do next. Suddenly, all the birds nearby stopped chirping. A sound off in the distance grew louder and louder and louder. It was the rumble of extremely large engines.

"How did the Cages get a crane and a bulldozer?" asked Mimi.

"It doesn't matter how they got them. What matters is that they did," replied a nervous Moto. "We have to figure out what we are going to do about it. And we better think of something fast, real fast before it is too late."

Out of the blue, an idea popped into Mimi's head, "Moto, I've got it! I've got it! We need to keep using what gorillas are afraid of."

"Great idea Mimi but besides zoos, what else are gorillas afraid of?" he asked.

Mimi quickly explained to him the four things that gorillas do not like: zoos, small insects, tiny animals, and rain.

"Last night, we scared them away with the zoo sign. Today, I think we need to try scaring them with something else," she added.

"Wait a second. You said gorillas are afraid of small insects, right? Would caterpillars count as small insects?" asked Moto.

"Yes, they would," confirmed Mimi. "It's super weird but funny at the same time. As large as gorillas are, they are terrified of small insects like caterpillars."

"Ok, cool. I've got an idea! Let's go. No time to waste," Moto exclaimed.

Mimi and Moto and Bella and Bailey jumped back on their motorcycles. They took off and headed down the dirt road towards the gorillas. Their knobby tires once again shot dirt and rocks behind their motorcycles. With her helmet glowing again, Mimi was the first to speak up.

"Moto, what exactly is your idea?"

"Operation Caterpillar. Trust me Mimi."

"I don't know exactly what you have in mind Moto, but I sure hope it works."

The four furry friends rode as fast as they could. They knew that the gorillas had started the crane and bulldozer. Luckily, cranes and bulldozers move slowly so catching them was not going to be difficult.

When they came to the end of the dirt road, Mimi and Moto could finally see the Cage's ugly little car. There was no sign of the gorillas. The four furry friends rode out to the middle of the paved road and skidded to a stop, kicking up dust everywhere. They shut off their motorcycles and their helmets stopped glowing instantly.

Down the road they could see the crane and bulldozer inching along slowly like two huge snails. Just as they had feared, the Cages were headed back around the mountain and towards the playground.

"Ok everyone, here is the plan. First, let's see if we can stop them by blocking the road. If that does not work, then we will have no choice but to try Operation Caterpillar," said Moto doing his best to sound confident.

Bella and Bailey looked at each other with raised eyebrows.

"Excuse me, but did you say Operation Caterpillar-meow?" asked Bella.

"You want to try stopping a huge crane and large bulldozer with itsy bitsy, teeny weeny, hairy, little caterpillars-woof?" added Bailey.

"No. We can't stop them with caterpillars," replied Moto. "But based on what Mimi told me, we can definitely scare them with caterpillars.

But first, let's try getting in front of them and blocking the road. Operation Caterpillar will be our last resort"

Mimi was looking towards the crane and bulldozer anxiously when she noticed something.

"Moto, look, on the left side over there. There is a small trail that runs along and just above the road. Do you see it? If we can get on it, I think we can get past the crane and bulldozer pretty easily."

"Great idea Mimi. Lead the way!"

Mimi and Moto and Bella and Bailey started their motorcycles again and Mimi took off first. She led them down the left side of the road towards the small trail she had spotted.

The trail Mimi had seen wasn't much of a trail at all. It was just a tiny path probably used by small animals. There was just enough room for their tires. It was also much bumpier than the trail over the mountain.

Once on it, their motorcycles and glowing

helmets bounced up and down again like bouncy balls. Mimi and Moto and Bella and Bailey held on tightly to their handlebars. Though their helmets were glowing, the four furry friends remained silent. Fortunately, the Cage's crane and bulldozer were moving slowly so they caught up to them quickly.

Mrs. Cage was driving the crane. She was behind Mr. Cage who was driving the bulldozer. She was the first to notice the four motorcycles on the path to her left. Even if she had wanted to shout to Mr. Cage, he would not have heard her. The crane and bulldozer engines were too loud.

When Mr. Cage noticed the motorcycles, he started pointing at them furiously. He began shouting. He was turning around and trying to get Mrs. Cage's attention back in the crane.

"Look! Look! It's the four motorcycle riders again. I knew I smelled something yucky and disgusting," he tried yelling over the loud and annoying engine noise.

From behind, Mrs. Cage could not hear a single word Mr. Cage had shouted. However, she could tell he was angry from the way his face looked when he turned around. His eyebrows were scrunched and slanting towards his eyes. His forehead had deep lines going across it. All of this made his face look like a fist again.

Mimi and Moto and Bella and Bailey quickly passed them. Once in front of the Cages, Mimi needed to find a way down to the road. Up ahead, she saw a small gully created by rainwater that led straight down to the pavement. There was no time to think. It was now or never.

"Follow me everyone!"

Mimi twisted her throttle, sped up, and guided her motorcycle down the gully to her right. Moto, Bella, and Bailey did the same. Their motorcycles navigated the uneven dirt gracefully and quickly. From the road, the Cages watched the four motorcyclists pull in front of them. They skidded to a quick stop, and then spun around to face the gorillas directly.

For the moment, the gorillas were forced to stop. When they did, Mr. Cage stood up in the bulldozer to get a better look. Behind him, Mrs. Cage stuck her head out the side window of the crane. While looking she was working hard to hide her smile. The bulldozer and crane engines continued to rumble loudly.

Without warning, Mimi and Moto and Bella and Bailey heard another noise. It sounded like a popcorn machine had turned on behind them. Brightly colored trails of smoke started to rain down from the sky. As each trail of smoke came down, there was a small popping sound and then a bright flash of light. Before they knew it, fourteen motorcycle riding raccoons had landed right behind them. The Bandits and Gazers had arrived to help.

The sight on the road was unbelievable. For the first time ever, the two monkeys, the cat, the dog, and the fourteen raccoons were face to face with the two gorillas. All of the animals remained silent. But the silence did not last long.

Mr. Cage began to roar and beat his chest with his fists. Behind him, Mrs. Cage tried to roar but kept laughing under her breath. Mimi and Moto and Bella and Bailey watched the gorillas. They revved their motorcycle engines loudly. The Bandits and Gazers did the same. All of them were confident they had stopped the gorillas.

But what happened next shocked all of them. The bulldozer and crane started to move forward again. The Cages were not stopping. They were heading straight at the motorcycles.

Like lead weights, Mimi and Moto's hearts sank to the bottom of their chests. They were afraid and thought they might have failed to protect the magical meteor made of motorcycles from the Cages.

CHAPTER 12

From the middle of the road Bailey barked out loudly, "It didn't work-woof! It didn't work-woof!"

"This is not good," shouted Mimi. "The gorillas are heading straight for us!"

"Yeah, I see that Mimi," shot back Moto.

"Is it time for Operation Caterpillar now?" she asked.

"You took the words right out of my mouth," answered Moto.

Mimi and Moto and Bella and Bailey quickly turned around and looked over their shoulders, as did the Bandits and Gazers. Off in the distance and over the trees, they could see sparks shooting even higher into the air. The magical meteor made of motorcycles seemed to be calling out for help.

"Mimi, tell the magical meteor made of motorcycles to stop sparking," yelled Moto.

"It doesn't matter anymore," she said, "I'm sure the Cages have already figured out that's where they need to go."

"Excuse me," chimed in Bella, "if we are going to try this Operation Caterpillar, won't we actually need some caterpillars-meow?"

"You are correct Bella, watch this," said Mimi, "Hey magical meteor made of motorcycles, this is Mimi. We need your help again fast, real fast. We want to scare the Cages with caterpillars, but we don't have time to find any. Can you help us?"

As soon as she finished talking, Bailey started barking. He was looking towards the forest on the side of the mountain. There was something flying towards them through the trees. It looked like a kaleidoscope of colors sailing through the leaves and branches. When it got closer, they could see that it was a flutter of butterflies. When the flutter got closer, they could see that each butterfly was also carrying a caterpillar.

With great care and skill, the butterflies flew out and gently placed the caterpillars on the handlebars of each motorcycle. When they were done, the flutter of butterflies disappeared back into the forest as quickly as they had appeared.

"How's that everyone?" asked Mimi

"Perfect, Mimi. Just perfect-meow," said Bella excitedly.

"But now what-bow-wow?" asked Bailey.

"Now it's time to really scare the Cages! For Operation Caterpillar to work, we'll need to fly right over the top of them," said Moto.

"And how are we going to do that?" asked Mimi.

"With a ramp, what else?" answered Moto.

"What ramp?" shouted Mimi loudly.

"Watch this and trust me Mimi," replied Moto.

He took a deep breath and started talking. "Hey magical meteor made of motorcycles. This is Moto. Thanks for the caterpillars. Now we need to jump over the top of the Cages for our plan to work. Can you get us a ramp?"

Almost instantly, Moto heard Bailey barking again. He knew this meant the dog saw something.

"Look up-woof! Look up-ruff!" barked Bailey.

Floating down from the great blue sky was a large wooden ramp. The ramp was being carried by four huge eagles. With their long and sharp talons, each eagle was holding a corner of it. The mighty birds swooped down and placed the ramp on the road halfway between the four furry friends and the Cages.

"Awesome job Moto. I think Operation Caterpillar just might work. Can I go first?"

begged Mimi eagerly.

"Yes you can. Send it Mimi!" yelled back Moto.

Mimi took off and rode straight at the ramp launching herself through the air. While sailing over the Cages, Mimi gently grabbed the caterpillar on her handlebars, dropped it, and yelled, "Wee! Here is a present for you, Mr. and Mrs. Cage!"

One by one, Moto and Bella and Bailey hit the ramp. They sailed through the air high over the Cages. The Bandits and Gazers did the same. Just like Mimi, all of them carefully dropped their caterpillar cargo onto the crane and bulldozer below.

Inside the crane and bulldozer, Mr. and Mrs. Cage started to hear noises above their heads. The sounds were soft and gentle. It was as if wet little cotton balls were raining down on them.

Mrs. Cage stuck her head out first to see what was going on. Sitting on top of her crane cab were caterpillars, lots and lots of hairy, little green caterpillars. Her eyes opened as wide as a gorilla's eyes could open. She screamed and without thinking, jumped out of the crane.

Mr. Cage heard Mrs. Cage scream. When he turned to look, he saw Mrs. Cage jump and land on the road. Not sure what was going on, Mr. Cage stuck his head out to look. As soon as he did, a caterpillar landed right on his nose. Not knowing what it was he grabbed it. When he realized what it was, he screamed even louder than Mrs. Cage. He threw the caterpillar down and jumped out of the bulldozer as quickly as he could.

Now behind the bulldozer and crane, Mimi and Moto and Bella and Bailey watched as the Cages panicked. The four furry friends quickly realized that the gorillas had not turned off the crane and bulldozer before jumping out.

With no one at the controls, the huge machines started to spin around uncontrollably.

The bulldozer swung around to the right. The crane swung around to the left. They collided with each other in the middle of the road causing a loud, screeching metal sound. The bulldozer started pushing the huge crane sideways toward the left side of the road where there was a cliff. In an instant, the crane disappeared over the edge.

With nothing left to push, the bulldozer followed the crane and drove itself over the edge too. A large cloud of dust rose up over the side of the road where the huge machines had tumbled down. Operation Caterpillar had worked.

CHAPTER 13

Mimi and Moto and Bella and Bailey stopped in the middle of the road and turned off their motorcycles. Excited that Operation Caterpillar was a success, the four furry friends high fived each other. But in their excitement, they had not noticed that the raccoons had disappeared.

"Where did the Bandits and Gazers go-meow?" asked Bella looking around.

"Look straight up-ruff," replied Bailey.

Above their heads were fourteen colored trails of smoke crisscrossing the great blue sky. Each one headed off in a different direction.

"Looks like once the raccoons dropped off

their caterpillars, their work helping us here was done," said Moto.

"Oh no! What about all the caterpillars?" shouted Mimi, startling everyone. She looked like she was going to cry while staring at the cloud of dust still rising up over the side of the road. Mimi was clearly afraid that protecting the magical meteor made of motorcycles may have harmed the caterpillars.

"Wait a minute, Mimi, look over there," replied a hopeful sounding Moto pointing at some trees.

The flutter of butterflies reappeared and came back out from the forest. They quickly flew over the road and disappeared into the still rising cloud of dust. After a few moments, the flutter of butterflies reappeared over the cliff. Each one was carrying a caterpillar.

"Oh, thank goodness. I feel much better now. It would have been awful if any of the caterpillars had been hurt," said a relieved sounding Mimi.

"On another note, look at that everybody," said Moto. He had turned around and was pointing down the road behind them.

The Cages were walking quickly towards their ugly little car. It was still parked on the side of the road where they had left it. In all of the chaos with the bulldozer and crane going over the cliff, the gorillas had managed to sneak by the four furry friends.

"What should we do about the gorillas-woof?" growled Bailey.

"I know what to do," said Mimi. She was looking up at the butterflies still hovering near the cliff. While the others watched, Mimi ran over to the edge of the road. She started pointing towards the gorillas and appeared to be talking to the flutter of butterflies. As she ran back towards Moto and Bella and Bailey, the butterflies flew down the road. They were heading straight for the Cages.

"Mimi, did you talk to the butterflies? What

did you say to them?" asked Moto.

"I asked if they could chase the gorillas away as far as possible. They said they can fly for days, and I said that would be perfect," she replied laughing.

The four watched as the flutter of butterflies flew silently towards the gorillas. The Cages did not notice them coming. Mrs. Cage was first to open the door to their ugly little car. "Dear, what are we going to do now?" she sighed.

"What do you think? We're going to head back to that playground. Do you think this little setback is going to stop a gorilla like me?" answered an irritated sounding Mr. Cage.

These were the last words he said before he noticed the flutter of butterflies right above his head. He froze in place and stared at them. Mrs. Cage looked at him and then she noticed the butterflies and froze in place too. The Cage's eyes opened wider and wider and wider. They could see that each butterfly was carrying something.

"No, no! Not again! No more caterpillars!" they screamed at the top of their lungs.

The gorillas quickly jumped into their ugly little car. Thick black smoke erupted from the back of it. The Cages sped away with the flutter of butterflies close behind. Mimi and Moto and Bella and Bailey watched as the ugly little car carrying the gorillas quickly disappeared over the horizon.

"I don't think we're going to see the Cages around here anymore," said Moto.

"But what if we do see the Cages again someday-meow?" asked the always curious Bella.

There was a moment of silence as each animal thought about this possibility. After a minute, it was Bailey who chimed in with another idea. It was an idea that was so wise, so brilliant, it would forever influence the four furry motorcycle riding friends.

"All animals should be encouraged to ride

motorcycles. If we see the gorillas again, we should try talking to them. Maybe we can convince them to ride with us too-ruff."

The four furry friends looked at each other. A smile broke out on each animals' face.

"What a brilliant idea Bailey. We are so lucky to have you and your champion's wisdom around," added Mimi. "Now let's ride back to the playground and check on the magical meteor made of motorcycles."

CHAPTER 14

"Wow-bow-wow," barked Bailey. He was looking down at himself and at his motorcycle. He was not sitting straight up on it like before. Instead, he had to lean forward to grab the handlebars.

During Operation Caterpillar, the four furry friends had not noticed that their motorcycles and gear had magically changed again.

Gone were the big fenders and knobby tires. Now their motorcycles were lower to the ground. They looked like little rockets. The tires were smoother and bigger. Their gear was different too. Now they had full body suits with large pads on the knees that looked like hockey pucks.

"These motorcycles look fast, real fast. I don't think it is going to take us too long to get back to the playground-meow," purred Bella.

"Let's ride," said a smiling Moto.

When they started up their new motorcycles, they sounded different and they sounded fast, real fast. Each of them had to wiggle their bottoms a little to get used to the new seats. Once settled in, they took off and headed back around the mountain.

Moto took the lead this time. He decided to take a different and slightly longer way back. He wasn't worried at all about getting lost. The magical meteor made of motorcycles was still shooting sparks high into the air. Whenever he did not know where to go, he just looked up and rode towards the sparks.

Mimi and Moto and Bella and Bailey rode fast, real fast. They felt the wind sweeping past them on their motorcycles. They leaned left.

They leaned right. Around some of the long and smooth curves, they even dragged their knees on the road.

Though their helmets were glowing again, the four furry friends did not talk while riding back to the playground. Each was thinking about all that had happened that day. And to be truthful, each of them was also completely enjoying their fast, new motorcycles.

When they arrived back at the playground, they parked right next to the magical meteor made of motorcycles. It was still sparking a little while they took off their gear.

It had been a long day for all of them. Mimi and Moto hopped up on the monkey bars. Swinging from their tails, they quietly ate some yummy, yellow bananas they had left on the playground bench. Bailey settled down underneath them and was chewing on a stick he had found. Bella curled up next to him and began licking her paws and cleaning her fur. Except for the occasional spark, the magical meteor made of motorcycles seemed to be resting too.

Mimi and Moto felt good back at the playground which felt like home. They were proud knowing that the magical meteor made of motorcycles was safe because they had helped to protect it. Even though they had only known the cat and dog for a few days, Bella and Bailey already felt like family. The monkeys were grateful they had met the Bandits and Gazers too. It felt good knowing they had friends who were around to help when they sometimes needed help the most.

For the moment, Mimi and Moto forgot about all of their questions. Where did the magical meteor made of motorcycles come from? Did someone or something send it? Why did it land here? Answering these questions would have to wait. For now, it was simply banana time.

The day could not have been going any better when out of the blue, Bailey perked up. He started sniffing the air. He looked up at the great blue sky and started to growl. Then he got up and started barking at it. Bella looked up trying to see what he was barking at. Mimi and Moto jumped down from the monkey bars and looked up too.

The four furry friends then heard a sound. It was the same sound they had heard the other day before their world had changed completely. There was no doubt about it. It was the unmistakable roar of motorcycles again. The sound kept getting louder and louder and louder. It got so loud that the trees nearby started shaking. Even the monkey bars started to rattle.

Then they saw it. Streaking high above their heads across the great blue sky was another magical meteor made of motorcycles. It disappeared over the horizon as the roar of motorcycles slowly faded away.

When the excitement was over, they turned around and looked at the first magical meteor

made of motorcycles. It was shooting off more sparks than ever before. It seemed happy as if a friend had shown up.

Mimi and Moto and Bella and Bailey looked at each other. No one needed to say a word. They put their motorcycle gear back on, jumped on their motorcycles, and rode off towards the horizon. The four furry friends knew what they had to do. They had to find and protect another magical meteor made of motorcycles.

THE END

About the Authors

Nancy Gerloff and Mark Augustyn, the Atlanta based wife and husband team behind Mimi and Moto, are on a mission to get children excited about motorcycles. Inspired by their daughter, the couple believes motorcycling makes children and their families happier, healthier, and much cooler. *Mimi and Moto's Magical Meteors: First Gear* is their first chapter book and follows up *The Adventures of Mimi and Moto* (2016) and *Mimi and Moto Ride the Alphabet* (2019). They plan to write more books, animate Mimi and Moto, and grow their brand internationally. Nancy and Mark hope you and the children in your life enjoy their newest, fastest, and most fun book yet! Visit them online at www.mimiandmoto.com and as always, ride safe.

Also Available:

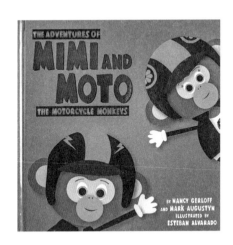

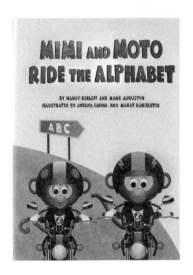